THE SELECTED
POETRY OF DAN PAGIS

D1614508

LITERATURE OF THE MIDDLE EAST

a series of fiction, poetry, and memoirs
in translation

Memoirs from the Women's Prison, by Nawal El Saadawi
translated by Marilyn Booth

Arabic Short Stories
translated by Denys Johnson-Davies

The Innocence of the Devil, by Nawal El Saadawi
translated by Sherif Hetata

Memory for Forgetfulness: August, Beirut, 1982
by Mahmoud Darwish
translated by Ibrahim Muhawi

Aunt Safiyya and the Monastery, by Bahaa' Taher
translated by Barbara Romaine

The Selected Poetry of Yehuda Amichai
newly revised and expanded edition
translated by Chana Bloch and Stephen Mitchell

The Selected Poetry of Dan Pagis
translated by Stephen Mitchell

THE
SELECTED
POETRY OF
DAN PAGIS

TRANSLATED BY
STEPHEN MITCHELL

WITH AN INTRODUCTION
BY ROBERT ALTER

University of California Press
Berkeley   Los Angeles   London

University of California Press
Berkeley and Los Angeles, California

University of California Press, Ltd.
London, England

Grateful acknowledgment is made to *The New Yorker*, for permission
to reprint "Ein Leben" and "A Moment at the Louvre"; to *Orim*, for
permission to reprint "Central Park, Twilight," "Outside an Air Base,
California," and "The Freedom Machine"; and to *Tikkun*, for permis-
sion to reprint "The Souvenir" and "Sominex."

Library of Congress Cataloging-in-Publication Data
Pagis, Dan.
    [Poems. English. Selections]
    The selected poetry of Dan Pagis / translated by Stephen Mitchell;
with an introduction by Robert Alter.
        p.   cm. — (Literature of the Middle East)
    Originally published: Variable directions. San Francisco :
North Point Press, 1989.
    ISBN 0-520-20539-1 (pbk. : alk. paper)
    1. Pagis, Dan—Translations into English.   I. Mitchell, Stephen,
1943– . II. Title. III. Series.
PJ5054.P32A25   1996
892'.416—dc20   96-14395
                                                    CIP

Printed in the United States of America
9 8 7 6 5 4 3 2 1

The paper used in this publication meets the minimum requirements
of American National Standard for Information Sciences—Perma-
nence of Paper for Printed Library Materials, ANSI Z39.48-1984.

I WOULD LIKE TO DEDICATE THIS BOOK
TO ESTHER AND MORRIS BIEDERMAN

S. M.

Contents

INTRODUCTION BY ROBERT ALTER   *xi*

GENEALOGY

Autobiography   5

Brothers   7

The Souvenir   9

Ein Leben   10

Homily   11

Siege   12

A LESSON IN OBSERVATION

The Last Ones   19

In the Laboratory   20

The Readiness   21

The Caveman Is Not about to Talk   22

A Lesson in Observation   23

Spaceship   24

Final Examination   25

TESTIMONY

Written in Pencil in the Sealed Railway-Car   29

An Opening to Satan   30

Europe, Late   31

The Roll Call   32

Testimony   33

Instructions for Crossing the Border   34

Draft of a Reparations Agreement   35

Footprints   36

CAMOUFLAGE

The Tortoise   45

A Modest Sum   46

Snake   47

Tidings   48

Bestiary   49

Writers   52

Tropical Greenhouse   54

Information   55

Real-Life Story   56

Twelve Faces of the Emerald   58

ENCOUNTERS

A Moment at the Louvre   63

Lament for a Master of Style   64

Encounters   65

Fragments of an Elegy   66

Twenty Years in the Valley   67

Jason's Grave in Jerusalem   68

An Ancient Complaint   69

Memorial Evening   70

Central Park, Twilight   71

The Grand Duke of New York   72

Early Winter, Long Island   74

The Deceased Writer: Photograph in the Rain   75

Moments of Old Age   76

The Portrait   77

THE ART OF CONTRACTION

A Small Poetics   81

Sugarduke   82

Wall Calendar   83
Final Report   84
For a Literary Survey   85
Silent Movie   86
The Art of Contraction   87
Sominex   88
Conversation   89
April   90
The End of Winter   91

TOWARD HOME

Acrobatics   95
Bridgehead Photograph   96
Devotion   98
For How Long   99
Out of Line   100
He'll Come Out for Sure   101
The Runner Artist   103
Picture Postcard from Our Youth   104
Toward Home   105
Outside an Air Base, California   106
A New Lover   107
Sudden Heart   108

THE FREEDOM MACHINE

Exposure   111
Point of Departure   112
The Limits of Physics   113
The Story   115
The Freedom Machine   116
How To   117

Recognition   118
Visit to a Physicist   119
Failure   120
Sport   121
Bisection   122
Wind from Variable Directions   123

PREVIOUS LIVES

Epilogue to Robinson Crusoe   131
The Tower   132
Pages in an Album   133
Seashell   134
Come   135
The Shot   136
The Beginning   137
The Cycle   138
Harvests   139
Ready for Parting   140
Scarabs   141
Already   142

BRAIN

Brain   145
End of the Questionnaire   153

ACKNOWLEDGMENTS   155

ABOUT THE AUTHOR   157

INTRODUCTION

ROBERT ALTER

It is a curious fact that the three leading Hebrew poets of the generation that began to publish shortly after the founding of the State of Israel were all born in German-speaking Europe—Dan Pagis in Bukovina, Yehuda Amichai in Bavaria, and Nathan Zach in Berlin. Of the three, Pagis's cultural displacement was the most drastic. Zach and Amichai both were brought to Palestine with their families in the mid-1930s, Zach at the age of five and Amichai at the age of twelve. Pagis did not reach Palestine until 1946, after having spent the first part of his adolescence in a Nazi concentration camp. The product of a Germanized Jewish home in what was once an eastern province of the Austro-Hungarian Empire, he probably never would have known Hebrew, never have had any serious connection with Israel or the Jewish cultural heritage, had he not been expelled from Europe by this ghastly spasm of historical violence and cast, for lack of any other haven, into the Middle East.

In the astonishing space of three or four years, he was publishing poetry in his newly learned language. This rapid determination to become a poet in Hebrew, I venture to guess, was not only a young person's willed act of adaptation but also the manifestation of a psychological need to seek expression in a medium that was itself a radical displacement of his native language. Displacement would remain a governing concept in Pagis's poetry, from the repeated and often flaunted effects of defamiliarization in his imagery, to his eerie refractions of the cataclysm that swept away European Jewry, to the global perspectives of his remarkable "evolutionary" and science-fiction poems, where time is accelerated, distorted, even reversed, and earthly existence is seen characteristically from an immense telescopic distance.

In stressing the role of Hebrew as the poet's linguistic medium of displacement, I do not mean to suggest that Pagis is estranged in any way from the language in which he writes. In fact, the revolution in Hebrew verse that he, Amichai, and Zach helped bring about was above all the perfection of a natural-sounding colloquial norm for Hebrew poetry. Perhaps it may have been easier for them to do this because as children suddenly called upon—by the inexorable pressure of their peer groups first of all—to possess a completely new linguistic competence, their primary associations were with the spoken language. Of the three, Pagis and Amichai make the most frequent efforts to incorporate elements of classical Hebrew in their predominantly colloquial diction, but in opposite ways—Amichai quite often imbedding allusive and ironically pointed bits of traditional texts in his own language, Pagis more unobtrusively modulating into locutions that recall in the Hebrew a higher literary decorum or, occasionally and somewhat distantly, a specific biblical or rabbinic text. As a poet, Pagis generally prefers contemporary vehicles and a contemporary sound, but it is also worth keeping in mind that the sixteen-year-old immigrant ignorant of Hebrew so thoroughly assimilated the rich classical tradition of the language that in his scholarly work he has become the foremost living authority on the poetics of Hebrew literature in the High Middle Ages and the Renaissance.

The experience of displacement that I have proposed as a key to Pagis's poetry is felt most pervasively in the brilliant obliquity of the stances he typically assumes. Again, the contrast with Amichai, who is so often confessional, autobiographical, vividly personal, is striking. There is a submerged freight of horror in a good deal of Pagis's work, but precisely because the historical occasion for it is so enormous, the way he finds to give it compelling expression without the shrillness of hysteria or the bathos of pseudoprophetic pronouncement is to cultivate a variety of distanced, ventriloquistic voices that become authentic surrogates for his own voice. When he writes a poem called "Autobiography," it is the autobiography of an archetype, Abel, the first victim; Abel is also, among many other avatars, Dan Pagis, 1939–45:

> you can die once, twice, even seven times,
> but you can't die a thousand times.
> I can.
> My underground cells reach everywhere.

In the poems that deal directly with genocide, this use of distanced and multiple voices is linked with an impulse to pull apart the basic categories of existence and reassemble them in strange configurations that expose the full depth of the outrage perpetrated. It is as though time and space (the affinity with the science-fiction poems is clear), man and God, self and other, body and soul, had been spun through a terrific centrifuge to be weirdly separated out, their positions disconcertingly reversed. The concluding stanza of "Testimony," to cite one of many memorable examples, extracts from its reconstitution of the cosmos an irony so comprehensive that it almost includes a note of consolation in its bitter dream of an encounter between wraithlike man and wraithlike God. The final clause of the poem turns dizzyingly on a verse from *Yigdal*, the medieval hymn based on Maimonides' Thirteen Principles, which declares that God "has no body [*guf*, rendered in the translation below as 'face'] nor the image of a body."

> And he in his mercy left nothing of me that would die.
> And I fled to him, floated up weightless, blue,
> forgiving—I would even say: apologizing—
> smoke to omnipotent smoke
> that has no face or image.

Odd as it may seem at first, Pagis is also a playful poet. The operation of this playfulness is perfectly continuous with the radical displacements of his more darkly brooding poems. The apparent contradiction here is readily resolved. If displacement has been one of the basic conditions of his own existence, the decision to make that condition into poetry was a way of converting it from a fate passively suffered into an imaginative ordering actively achieved. The same poetic force that juggles ontological categories in the Holocaust poems, transforming Creator and victim alike into faceless smoke, or a fleeing refugee into "imaginary man" (in "Instructions for Crossing the Border"), is also behind the metamorphosis of armchairs and balloons into strange and wonderful animals in the delightful group of poems, "Bestiary." The oddest animal of the bestiary is, of course, that predatory biped who "alone/cooks animals, peppers them." But this oddness is only the reverse, witty side of the perception in the Holocaust poems of something radically uncanny about man— abysmally so when he puts on boots and marches people into box-cars, astonishingly so when as victim he manages, despite everything, to survive. In "Bestiary," however, the oddness of the human animal produces a kind of existential comedy:

. . . he alone laughs,
and, strangest of all, rides of his own free will
on a motorcycle.
He has four limbs,
two ears,
a hundred hearts.

Another relatively late poem, "Jason's Grave in Jerusalem," is a striking illustration of these metamorphic powers of imagination, of how the once-displaced person has become an artificer of suggestive displacements. Jason's tomb really exists in the midst of a prosperous residential neighborhood in Jerusalem, a city where the living and the dead are in any case mingled promiscuously through architecture, topography, and archaeological remains surrounded by urban bustle. This is one of the rare poems in which Pagis actually introduces an explicit element of the Israeli landscape; characteristically, he spins out of this Jerusalem burial chamber dug into the living rock an imaginative credenza in which land and sea, incarceration and flight, the contemporary and the archaic, life and death, myth and actuality, spiral around each other in a lovely dance.

The Hellenistic Jason of the Judean King Yannai's court blends into the legendary Jason pursuing the golden fleece. The catalyst for this and all the other transformations of the poem is the image of a ship scratched on the wall of the tomb—in effect, an emblem inscribed within the poem's imagined world of the magical property of artifice to become a vehicle of escape from the constraints of the quotidian, from what Pagis elsewhere calls "the limits of physics." The golden fleece seized by this Jason, as we learn in the last three lines, turns out to be the sheer sensuous splendor of the Mediterranean world through which the fabled hero glides. In the

Hebrew, that climactic sensuousness is made palpable in the rich play of alliteration and assonance through which the concluding nine words of the poem are finely interwoven: *shémesh shel máyim/méshi shel rúah/sháyish shel kétzef*. No translation could reproduce just that effect, but here as elsewhere, the resourcefulness and sensitivity of Stephen Mitchell's version are remarkable. For Pagis's poetry is not only wry and shrewdly colloquial (qualities more readily translatable into contemporary English), but it also on occasion delights in the texture of language and the feel of experience this texture is made to match. For that quality, too, Stephen Mitchell has fashioned eminently workable English equivalents. Thus, at the end of "Jason's Grave in Jerusalem," Pagis's antique sailor is said to smuggle, "with great profit . . . very expensive merchandise." And now those last three lines in English:

> sunlight of water,
> velvet of sea-breeze,
> marble of foam.

Some English discussions of Pagis's work have tended to pigeonhole him as a "poet of the Holocaust," but in fact his imaginative landscape extends from the grim vistas of genocide to the luminous horizon of medieval Hebrew poetry in the Iberian peninsula. He is, after all, the gifted expositor of Moses Ibn Ezra, Judah Halevi, Solomon Ibn Gabirol, and the other great poets of the eleventh and twelfth centuries who responded so richly to the colors and images and aesthetic values of worldly existence, who celebrated in the intricate, formal artifice of their verse the abiding power of art. Pagis's own poetry, of course, is necessarily more understated and more conversational than the medieval texts he has studied, but in its distinctively modern idiom it, too, is a self-conscious demonstration and affirmation of what the poetic imagination can do.

The Selected
Poetry of Dan Pagis

GENEALOGY

AUTOBIOGRAPHY

I died with the first blow and was buried
among the rocks of the field.
The raven taught my parents
what to do with me.

If my family is famous,
not a little of the credit goes to me.
My brother invented murder,
my parents invented grief,
I invented silence.

Afterward the well-known events took place.
Our inventions were perfected. One thing led to another,
orders were given. There were those who murdered in their own
        way,
grieved in their own way.

I won't mention names
out of consideration for the reader,
since at first the details horrify
though finally they're a bore:

you can die once, twice, even seven times,
but you can't die a thousand times.
I can.
My underground cells reach everywhere.

When Cain began to multiply on the face of the earth,
I began to multiply in the belly of the earth,
and my strength has long been greater than his.
His legions desert him and go over to me,
and even this is only half a revenge.

BROTHERS

1

Abel was blond and woolly
and looked as humble
as the softest of his little goats
and curled like the smoke of the offering
that he sent up
to the nose of his lord.
Cain was straight: like a knife.

2

Cain is dumbstruck. His large hand
gropes in the slaughtered throat in front of him:
where has this silence burst from?

3

Abel remains in the field. Cain remains Cain. And since it was de-
creed that he is to be a wanderer, he wanders diligently. Each morn-
ing he changes horizons. One day he discovers: the earth tricked him
all those years. *It* had moved, while he, Cain, had walked on one
spot. Had walked, jogged, run, on a single piece of ground exactly as
big as his sandals.

4

On an evening of mercy he happens upon
a convenient haystack.
He sinks in, is swallowed, rests.
Shhh, Cain is asleep.
Smiling, he dreams that he is his brother.

5

Do not be afraid.
It has been decreed that whoever kills you
shall be punished sevenfold.
Your brother Abel guards you from all harm.

The Souvenir

The town where I was born, Radautz, in the county of Bukovina, threw me out when I was ten. On that day she forgot me, as if I had died, and I forgot her too. We were both satisfied with that.

Forty years later, all at once, she sent me a souvenir. Like an unpleasant aunt whom you're supposed to love just because she is a blood relative. It was a new photograph, her latest winter portrait. A canopied wagon is waiting in the courtyard. The horse, turning its head, gazes affectionately at an elderly man who is busy closing some kind of gate. Ah, it's a funeral. There are just two members left in the Burial Society: the gravedigger and the horse.

But it's a splendid funeral; all around, in the strong wind, thousands of snowflakes are crowding, each one a crystal star with its own particular design. So there is still the same impulse to be special, still the same illusions. Since all snow-stars have just one pattern: six points, a Star of David in fact. In a minute they will all start melting and turn into a mass of plain snow. In their midst my elderly town has prepared a grave for me too.

EIN LEBEN

In the month of her death, she is standing by the windowframe,
a young woman with a stylish, permanent wave.
She seems to be in a contemplative mood
as she stands there looking out the window.

Through the glass an afternoon cloud of 1934
looks in at her, blurred, slightly out of focus,
but her faithful servant. On the inside
I'm the one looking at her, four years old almost,

holding back my ball, quietly
going out of the photo and growing old,
growing old carefully, quietly,
so as not to frighten her.

Homily

From the start, the forces were unequal: Satan a grand seigneur in heaven, Job mere flesh and blood. And anyway, the contest was unfair. Job, who had lost all his wealth and had been bereaved of his sons and daughters and stricken with loathsome boils, wasn't even aware that it was a contest.

Because he complained too much, the referee silenced him. So, having accepted this decision, in silence, he defeated his opponent without even realizing it. Therefore his wealth was restored, he was given sons and daughters—new ones, of course—and his grief for the first children was taken away.

We might imagine that this retribution was the most terrible thing of all. We might imagine that the most terrible thing was Job's ignorance: not understanding whom he had defeated, or even that he had won. But in fact, the most terrible thing of all is that Job never existed and was just a parable.

SIEGE

1

Cloister gardens, secluded, and poppies: a drowsy noon.
Here, aside from myself, there is just one man in the sun.
Who is it, why it's my neighbor, the prominent dirt contractor.
I'm very glad that we met, he says from inside his skull,
but right now I'm in a hurry. We're digging in. Catch you later.

2

Suddenly the hoopoe. Sudden, motionless.
A tuft of feathers motionless. An edge of fence.
The eye wide open, a black mirror
for the soul beyond.
Suddenly it flies: to the pine tree
over the wall.
The moment
created from nothing, swallowed up in nothing.
The pine tree is empty.

3

The first burial was in the dust,
beneath the track of legions.
The second burial, of gathered bones,
was in a secret ossuary carved in limestone.
Now, at the close of some century, in the flaming noon,
the ossuary is empty.
The third burial is in the wind.

4

There is time enough for us, this mosaic floor and me.
I was born under the sign of Libra,
it was born under the whole zodiac:
all matters of chance are included in it,
it has all the signs. There is time enough.
Both of us, slowly, are crumbling.
The little stone cubes that have broken off, scattered,
freed from destiny, are ready
for the game of chance.
Here is one cube: smooth, intact, a die
with every surface empty.
I pick it up,
aim at the center of the mosaic,
make a bet, shoot.
Zero: I won.

5

Red into black. Wild demonstrations of poppies
break ranks quietly and fall. The seeds,
trapped, lie in hiding.
And meanwhile Summer, a young tyrant,
drafts the thorns of the globe thistles.
The forces are even. Soon
bare feet in the fields. Soon,
inevitably: the scorpion.

6

There at the gate, between stone columns,
something turns white, flickers.

Signals from whom,
a flag for what kind of surrender?
An old newspaper, this morning's, hugs the wall,
tries to sneak off, is captured.
The front-page headlines are carved
in the limestone.

7

From the monastery tower
the antenna of the cross
broadcasts the afternoon news, first the top story:
The third burial is in the wind.
The fertile dust returns, covering the land.
The second burial was in the limestone.
Nearby, a stone's-throw away, stands
the city, an engraved ossuary.
The first burial was in the dust.

8

Well then, the armies have dug in. The front line runs crisscross.
If I wander right or left
I'll step on a skull: everything is mined.

9

I can see now: the forces are even.
Who will attack first, who will surprise whom?
From the blind spot on the slope I hear
a tired shifting of gears:
the present moment is coming up from the plain
in a pincer-movement maneuver.
The siege tightens.

10

I report: the equipment is in perfect condition.
Ten years or twenty after I fell
in our victorious battle against Emperor Titus
someone came, perhaps my orphan,
and reverently gathered my bones
(as it is written: "a day of rejoicing for him"),
arranged them nicely in the ossuary,
little ones here, big ones there, and at the top, the skull.
He covered them, sealed the emergency depot,
disguised it as dust. Since then
I am in constant readiness.
And so in this emergency the equipment is ready,
the command has been verified: I gather myself, lift my bones,
put on skin and muscles, my full-dress uniform,
and report to the regiment
right now, in the end of days.

Author's Notes

Section 1: A kind of poppy, *papaver somniferum*, is used to produce opium. This section is written in classical hexameter verse, as are several tombstone inscriptions in Palestine from the period of the Second Temple and after its destruction.

Section 3: "At first they would bury them in pits. After the flesh had decayed, they would gather up the bones and bury them in ossuaries. That day was a day of mourning; the next, a day of rejoicing, because their ancestors would now protect them from the divine wrath." (Palestinian Talmud, Mo'ed Katan 1,5)

Section 10: "Rabbi Meir said, 'When one gathers up the bones of his father and mother, it is a day of rejoicing.'" (Mishnah, Mo'ed Katan 1,5)

"Unclassified. Upon receiving this command you must report for active duty at the assigned position of your unit. Bring with you all the military equipment you have in your possession." (Israeli government form for calling up the army reserves)

"Then the land shall give back the dead which it receives today for safekeeping, and nothing at all shall be changed in their appearance." (The Book of Barukh, 5,2)

A LESSON IN
OBSERVATION

THE LAST ONES

I am already quite scarce. For years
I have appeared only here and there
at the edges of this jungle. My graceless body,
well camouflaged among the reeds, clings
to the damp shadow around it.
Had I been civilized,
I would never have been able to hold out.
I am tired. Only the great fires
still drive me from hidingplace to hidingplace.

And what now? My fame is only in the rumors
that from time to time
and even from hour to hour
I'm shrinking.
But it is certain that at this very moment
someone is tracking me. Cautiously
I prick all my ears and wait. The steps
already rustle the dead leaves. Very close. Here.
Is this it?

Am I it? I am.
There is no time to explain.

In the Laboratory

The data in the glass beaker: a dozen scorpions
of various species—a swarming, compromising
society of egalitarians. Trampling and trampled upon.
Now the experiment: an inquisitive creator blows
the poison gas inside
and immediately
each one is alone in the world,
raised on its tail, stiff, begging the glass wall
for one more moment.
The sting is already superfluous;
the pincers do not understand;
the straw body waits for the final shudder.
Far away, in the dust, the sinister angels
are startled.
It's only an experiment. An experiment. Not a judgment
of poison for poison.

THE READINESS

I too, like all the apes in the neighborhood,
grumble from branch to branch:
the past age, which was filled with sun, has passed.
Now it's cold. The nuts are too hard.
The carnivores are getting more and more supple.

This is it, I'm emigrating. Good-bye.

Hey, what's happening,
my tongue's tied in knots,
my shoulders, where are my shoulders,
suddenly I've got stature,
erectness,
suddenly I'm threatened with
what, a high brow!
Bulbs, flickering bulbs.

How good this silence is. I'm almost, almost perfected.
I pick out an attractive suit,
get dressed,
light up a cigarette, slowly,
and sit down with the stopwatch, my only friend,
beside the table, in perfect readiness
for the invention of chess.

The Caveman Is Not about to Talk

At time's tail end, my great-grandchildren's great-
Grandchildren pause,
My skull in hand, and try to calculate
The centuries I ground between my jaws.

And what news of the mammoth will they wrest
From my laconic mouth? I've got time:
I'm not about to talk. They haven't guessed
My profile, even. Fine,

Let them enjoy the bones that I bequeath
In a clump of dust. But if they looked beneath:
Here I am,

Still in my cave, complexion like a baby's,
Pink and soft and wonderfully at ease,
Never expelled from Mama's cozy womb.

A LESSON IN OBSERVATION

Pay close attention: the world that appears now
at zero-point-zero-one degrees
was, as far as is known,
the only one
that burst out of the silence.

It hovered within a blue bubble, fairly large;
and sometimes there were clouds, sea breezes,
sometimes a house, perhaps a kite, children,
and here and there an angel,
or a garden, or a town.
Beneath these were the dead, beneath them
rock, beneath this the fiery prison.

Is that clear? I will repeat: outside there were
clouds, screams, air-to-air missiles,
fire in the fields, memory.
Far beneath these, there were houses, children. What else?

The little dot on the side? It seems to be
the only moon of that world.
It blew itself out even before this.

SPACESHIP

Soon I will have to begin. All around me
moons have lit up. Have burned.
I am receiving a different light, perhaps from inside,
like a dim streetlamp
in a city park I once heard of.
And I try to imagine: a city. How was a city possible,
for example? What were the prerequisites
for a tree? For the growth of a bench? For a child?

Now to take off.
There is no time left.
I am preparing myself
to hover over the face of the non-abyss
into my body and onward

FINAL EXAMINATION

"If I am not mistaken:
the lightning that disappeared
only now pierces
the eye.
The air that has taken the place
of the severed hand hurts
the cripple."

    —No, that is not right. Memory is not there.
    What you said is only a parable.
    But you, my servant, you
    must be precise. I expected more from you.
    It doesn't matter. Do not fear, my servant. You will not fail.
    Think. Think again, well, and answer me:
    Where is memory?
    Who has pierced?
    What was severed?

TESTIMONY

WRITTEN IN PENCIL
IN THE SEALED RAILWAY-CAR

here in this carload
i am eve
with abel my son
if you see my other son
cain son of man
tell him that i

An Opening to Satan

As he waited in front of the new invention,
Danton said, "The verb *to guillotine*
(this brand-new verb of ours) is limited
in the tenses and persons of its conjugation:
for example, I shall not have a chance to say
I was guillotined."

Acute and poignant, that sentence, but naive.
Here am I (and I'm nobody special),
I was beheaded
I was hanged
I was burned
I was shot
I was massacred.
I was forgotten.
(But why give an opening to Satan?—
he might still recall
that, morally at least,
for the time being, I've won.)

EUROPE, LATE

Violins float in the sky,
and a straw hat. I beg your pardon,
what year is it?
Thirty-nine and a half, still awfully early,
you can turn off the radio.
I would like to introduce you to:
the sea breeze, the life of the party,
terribly mischievous,
whirling in a bell-skirt, slapping down
the worried newspapers: tango! tango!
And the park hums to itself:
      I kiss your dainty hand, madame,
      your hand as soft and elegant
      as a white suede glove. You'll see, madame,
      that everything will be all right,
      just heavenly—you wait and see.
      No, it could never happen here,
      don't worry so—you'll see—it could

THE ROLL CALL

He stands, stamps a little in his boots,
rubs his hands. He's cold in the morning breeze:
a diligent angel, who worked hard for his promotions.
Suddenly he thinks he's made a mistake: all eyes,
he counts again in the open notebook
all the bodies waiting for him in the square,
camp within camp: only I
am not there, am not there, am a mistake,
turn off my eyes, quickly, erase my shadow.
I shall not want. The sum will be all right
without me: here forever.

Testimony

No no: they definitely were
human beings: uniforms, boots.
How to explain? They were created
in the image.

I was a shade.
A different creator made me.

And he in his mercy left nothing of me that would die.
And I fled to him, floated up weightless, blue,
forgiving—I would even say: apologizing—
smoke to omnipotent smoke
that has no face or image.

Instructions for
Crossing the Border

Imaginary man, go. Here is your passport.
You are not allowed to remember.
You have to match the description:
your eyes are already blue.
Don't escape with the sparks
inside the smokestack:
you are a man, you sit in the train.
Sit comfortably.
You've got a decent coat now,
a repaired body, a new name
ready in your throat.
Go. You are not allowed to forget.

Draft of a
Reparations Agreement

All right, gentlemen who cry blue murder as always,
nagging miracle-makers,
quiet!
Everything will be returned to its place,
paragraph after paragraph.
The scream back into the throat.
The gold teeth back to the gums.
The terror.
The smoke back to the tin chimney and further on and inside
back to the hollow of the bones,
and already you will be covered with skin and sinews and you will
    live,
look, you will have your lives back,
sit in the living room, read the evening paper.
Here you are. Nothing is too late.
As to the yellow star:
it will be torn from your chest
immediately
and will emigrate
to the sky.

FOOTPRINTS

From heaven to the heaven of heavens to the heaven of night

YANNAI

Against my will
I was continued by this cloud: restless, gray,
trying to forget in the horizon, which always receded

Hail falling hard,
like the chatter of teeth:
refugee pellets pushing eagerly
into their own destruction

In another sector
clouds not yet identified.
Searchlights that set up
giant crosses of light
for the victim.
Unloading of cattle cars.

Afterward the letters fly up,
after the flying letters mud
hurries, snuffs, covers for a time

It's true, I was a mistake, I was forgotten
in the sealed car, my body tied up
in the sack of life

Here's the pocket where I found bread,
sweet crumbs, all from the same world

Maybe there's a window here—if you don't mind,
look near that body, maybe you can open up
a bit. That reminds me
(pardon me) of the joke about the two Jews
in the train, they were traveling to

Say something more; talk.
Can I pass from my body and onward—

*

From heaven to the heaven of heavens to the heaven of night
long convoys of smoke

The new seraphim who haven't yet understood,
prisoners of hope, astray in the empty freedom,
suspicious as always: how to exploit
this sudden vacuum, maybe
the double citizenship will help,
the old passport,
maybe the cloud? what's new in the cloud,
here too of course
they take bribes. And between us: the biggest bills
are still nicely hidden away, sewn
between the soles—
but the shoes have been piled up below:
a great gaping heap

Convoys of smoke. Sometimes
someone breaks away,
recognizes me for some reason, calls my name.

And I put on a pleasant face, try to remember:
who else
who

Without any right to remember, I remember
a man screaming in a corner, bayonets rising
to fulfill their role
in him

Without any right to remember. What else
was there? Already I'm not afraid
that I might say

without any connection at all:
there was a heart, blue from excessive winter,
and a lamp, round, blue, kindhearted.
But the kerosene disappears with the blood, the flame flickers—

Yes, before I forget:
the rain stole across some border, so did I,
on forbidden escape routes, with forbidden hope,
we both passed the mouth of the pits

Maybe now
I'm looking in that rain
for the scarlet thread

Where to begin?
I don't even know how to ask.
Too many tongues are mixed in my mouth. But

at the crossing of these winds,
very diligent, I immerse myself
in the laws of heavenly grammar: I am learning
the declensions and ascensions of
silence.

> *Who has given you the right to jest?*
> *What is above you you already know.*
> *You meant to ask about what is within you,*
> *what is abysmally through you.*
> *How is it that you did not see?*

But I didn't know I was alive.
From the heaven of heavens to the heaven of night
angels rushed, sometimes one of them
would look back, see me, shrug his shoulders,
continue from my body and onward

*

Frozen and burst, clotted,
scarred,
charred, choked.

If it has been ordained that I pull out of here,
I'll try to descend rung by rung,
I hold on to each óne, carefully—
but there is no end to the ladder, and already
no time. All I can still do is fall
into the world

And on my way back
my eyes hint to me:
you have been, what more did you want to see?
Close us and see:
you are the darkness, you are the sign.

And my throat says to me:
if you are still alive, give me an opening, I
must praise.

And my upside-down head is faithful to me,
and my hands hold me tight:
I am falling   falling
from heaven to the heaven of heavens to the heaven of night

*

Well then: a world.
The gray is reconciled by the blue.
In the gate of this cloud, already a turquoise
innocence, perhaps light green. Already sleep.
Heavens renew themselves, try out their wings, see me

and run for their lives. I no longer wonder.
The gate bursts open:
a lake
void   void   pure of reflections

Over there,
in that arched blue, on the edge of the air,

I once lived. My window was fragile.
Maybe what remained of me
were little gliders that hadn't grown up:
they still repeat themselves in still-clouds, glide,
slice the moment
      (not to remember now, not to remember)

And before I arrive
      (now to stretch out to the end, to stretch out)
already awake, spread to the tips of my wings,
against my will I feel that, very near,
inside, imprisoned by hopes, there flickers
this ball of the earth,
scarred, covered with footprints.

CAMOUFLAGE

THE TORTOISE

You're quick on your light feet, Achilles.
I am very very slow.
That's why I'm famous.

The distance between us grows smaller and smaller
but doesn't vanish.
You'll never catch up.

Keep straining so hard, mon cher, and you'll die young.
I, old beyond age,
waddle around the world.

I confess: being a champion,
an eternal victor in the dust—
this is a heavy burden.

I'm considering:
perhaps I should grow wings.

A Modest Sum

Our forefathers the tortoise and the sea lizard tramped
Ponderously through the tepid comfort of the swamp.
Their merit did not save us. The jungle climbed,
Spread, burst, and was swept away, a sign of the times.
My teacher, the gorilla, is severe; does not approve
That I'm a modest youngster, considerate, well-behaved.
Every time I'm terrified by the blood or pain,
He shouts: what's wrong with you, when will you be a man!
He's right: I should develop, shouldn't ponder
So much. Should be a well-adjusted hunter.

SNAKE

The sand is swift, overflowing,
burrowing inside itself, searching
for remnants, tombstones, ancestors'
bones.
I never understood this hunger
for the past. I
am a series of instants,
shed my skin with ease,
forget,
outsmart myself.
In all this desert only I can guess
who was who.

TIDINGS

The great fish that vomited out Jonah
swallowed nothing more.
Without any prophecy in his guts, he pined away.

The great fish died and the sea vomited him out onto dry land,
three hundred cubits of disappointed and forsaken flesh
in the light of the end of day.

Then they were merciful to him, an omen of things to come in a
        moment:
gangs of crabs
surrounded him, delighted in him, picked him clean.

After all the tidings, there remained on the deserted beach
the skeleton: caverns, columns, gates, secret entranceways—
a city of refuge for an escaped wind. Everything has been fulfilled.

Bestiary

The Elephant

The elephant, a crusty old general, scarred,
patient, thick-skinned:
on his pillarlike legs stands a whole world
of belly. But
he is so strong
that he conquers himself
through himself: at zero hour,
with cotton-puff caution,
with love dependent on nothing,
he steps
on sixteen marvelously accurate wristwatches,
ties four on each foot like skates
and glides forth smoothly
out of his elephant fate.

Armchairs

The slowest animals
are the soft large-eared leather armchairs
that wait in the corners of hotel lobbies.
They multiply
in the shade of potted philodendrons.
And though content to live
more slowly than elephants,
they are always just about
to leave on a secret, end-
less safari.

Fossils

They are all unparalleled deniers,
these creatures that go on living forever.
The royal arch-fly frozen in amber
scorns time and with a thousand eyes
takes his nap in the sun.
The arch-shell is an ear that refuses to listen.
The arch-fish renounced even himself
and left just the imprint of his bones in the rock.
The paragon of creation among the fossils
is the Venus of Milo,
she who forever abstains
with arms of air.

Balloons

Balloons at parties fondle one another
between paper serpents
and humbly accept
their limit, the ceiling of the room.
They are ready for any hint,
willing to obey the slightest breeze.
But even the eternally humble must come
to their appointed end.
The soul suddenly leaks out
in a terrified whistle
or explodes
with a single pop.
Afterward the rubber bodies
languish
on the edges of a filthy rug,

and the souls wander
through the in-between world just about
as high as your nose.

The Biped

The biped is quite a strange creature:
through his flesh he is related
to the other predatory animals, but he alone
cooks animals, peppers them,
he alone is clothed with animals, shod in animals,
he alone thinks
that he's a stranger in the world, alone protests
against what is decreed, he alone laughs,
and, strangest of all, rides of his own free will
on a motorcycle.
He has four limbs,
two ears,
a hundred hearts.

WRITERS

I've written many words in my life. Words of evasion or honesty, a half-truth here and there, or a truth and a half, good ones and bad ones, etc. All this is, of course, pure supposition, since like all other fountain pens I have no memory. I don't need one either: I come from an old, highly respected firm, Mont Blanc, which demands nothing of me except nobility. Only blue blood flows to my 14-karat nib. I live in harmony with the select sheet of paper, with the light pressure between thumb and index finger. Sometimes, in the midst of ponderings, I even rise to the forehead and rest upon it for a moment or two.

The modern era hurt me, as it did all members of the nobility. Already years ago (of course, I can't remember when) that fool rushed in, that vulgar plastic Bic-stick, that headstrong round-pated ballpoint. It doesn't have even one drop of real blood, just a kind of sticky chemical mucous that destroys the pocket. And the typewriter, that chatterbox. She ties the letters to thin skewers that flail inside her belly like spider legs. Now she has been empowered with electricity, beautified with all kinds of gadgetry, and even so she's becoming unfashionable. Cosmetics won't help her.

These two, whatever chutzpah they may have, at least admit that they are living a temporary life: they write and forget. But the word processor—mere sleight of hand! This acrobat makes a pretense of remembering, of collecting thousands of words in his guts. At the push of a button, he vomits them all onto the screen, surrenders them to any twist, to any arbitrary change, and does not remember the faithfulness of their youth, not even for a moment. This isn't memory, it's forgery! And why am I not furious? Because they will rise up against him too, the crook, he too will be forgotten, like all writers, like me.

TROPICAL GREENHOUSE

Counterfeit Eden,
cunning cage of blossoming.

The glass walls pretend they're
air African rubber fans drip calla
gape from everywhere the cobra
ficus twists and the moths
lured by the brown-purple orchids of Hades
dip a thousand long tongues into the dark nectar.

But outside, free,
in a bare field,
camouflaged by the color of flesh,
straight, thin,
the You-Me is flowering,
a Mediterranean androgyne,
the You-Me, the only
one of its kind.

INFORMATION

And what's new on the beach? A twisted path
left by the sand snake.
A shelter for the hermit crab who with his body
furnished an empty conch, since it's a good life
in the house of the dead.
A heavy boot.
Sudden extinction steps toward the anthill.

And what's new on the beach? A giant shell
floats and bursts open: Aphrodite is born in the foam,
oh wonderful flesh.
At full sail, Alexander's mighty fleet passes by,
to conquer the world.
The remains of a tank-tread
are turning into a dinosaur's spine.
An F-15 takes off, becomes obsolete,
is gone.

And what's new on the beach? A twisted path
left by the sand snake.

REAL-LIFE STORY

The foot is growing old.
She has gone through a lot, gone over a lot:
all those confused steps—
only here and there a step that was correct
between miles of nothing.

She has had enough.
She prays for a humble miracle, without any drama:
not walking on water,
not stepping in the midst of fire,
just a quiet condominium, with a partner who is a mensch,
and with a steady pension.

She has had so many disappointments. The cement-tile floor,
the native son who made her happy in the summer heat,
grew slippery, evasive,
cold and alien to her in winter.
The hairy carpet, a new immigrant from Tashkent,
would amuse her, tickle her a little,
but when she moved, he forgot her right away.

Not to worry! Finally the foot meets
a nice gray middle-aged sock,
a veteran from the garment district, and lo and behold
he gives her abundant warmth,
hugs her, and sings her a little silent song:

"You fill me up completely,
and I accept you just the way you are.
I fit you perfectly, dear foot,
from your dried-up toe
to your hurt Achilles' heel.
Soon we'll find a nice shoe
big enough for both of us,
and every evening we'll move
to our second home, a comfortable slipper."

TWELVE FACES OF THE EMERALD

1

I am exceedingly green: chillgreen.
What have I to do
with all the greenishness of chance?
I am the green-source,
the green-self,
one and incomparable.

2

The most suspicious flash
in the cat's eye
at the most acute moment
aspires
to be
me.

3

What have I to do with you, or the living grass?
Among you I am a stranger—
brilliant, cold, playing with my eternities.

4

The emperor Nero, artist in stage lighting,
raises me to his red eye:
only my green can pacify his blood.
Through me he observes the end of the burning world.

5

Slander! I am not
envious of the diamond: fickle duke,
reckless, lacking in self-control:
daggers! fireworks!
I, on the contrary, am moderate,
know how to bide my time,
to pour, green and accurate,
the poison.

6

As if I shared a secret. Shade of blue,
hint of red in a polished facet,
hesitating violet—
they're gone, they're gone.
I, the green-source,
abolish the colors of the rainbow.

7

You think that you will find your image
in mine.
No. I shall not leave a trace of you;
you never were in me.
Mirror facing mirror facing mirror, enchanted,
I am reflected in I.

8

With one flick of the hand
I smash your days into twelve
green nights.

9

I am all eye.
I shall never sleep.

10

And so I put on a face,
twelve facets apparently transparent.

11

Fragments of light:
they indeed are my soul: I shall not fear.
I shall not die.
I have no need to compromise.

12

You will never find the secret of my power.
I am I: crystallized carbon
with a very small quantity
of chromium oxide.

ENCOUNTERS

A Moment at the Louvre

I'm hurrying to an urgent appointment:
inside the glass case, waiting for me
(I'm already late) is Pharaoh's quick scribe.
He is seated with legs crossed.
Absolutely attentive,
he looks at me with white eyes.
What shall I dictate to him.
What must I dictate to him.

Visitors casually stroll by, stop for a moment,
are reflected in the glass case, are erased.

Well then, the two of us.
His knees look at me with great patience.
Well then, what.
He is burnt clay,
I am clay that is gradually hardening.
What shall I bequeath him.

He sees
my silence,
carves it
onto his clean slate.

I peek at the clock, am gradually erased
from the glass, from his presence.
He didn't see that I already was.
He is waiting for me.
I am already late.

LAMENT FOR A MASTER OF STYLE

He was always hunting for the *mot juste*. It would always elude him, leap up from between his fingers like a grasshopper. And since he never gave up, it finally took its revenge: a dark cloud rose on the horizon, myriads of grasshoppers, ravenous words that swarmed over his books, his face, his mouth, and left them desolate.

ENCOUNTERS

You encounter a mirror and look away too late.
What's new, you haven't changed at all! Good-bye, good-bye.

You meet, almost in secret, a bundle of old papers.
You survived, they did too. What else can you say?

You wander about in veins, in arteries, to the heartbeat, then
to a different beat. This blood too is gone.

And suddenly, in the drawer, the photograph: you,
the protruding face-bones, the astonished look,

yes, the same bones. Now you understand:
you didn't even die. You renounced in vain.

And what answer will you return with? since there is no question.
You're ready for the encounter, rise and break open the door

and climb down the cellar stairs and introduce yourself to the wall.

FRAGMENTS OF AN ELEGY

I've closed your eyes.
I've returned your hands to their place.
The soles of your feet look at me with pity:
I am superfluous.
Now I find my hands.
What shall I do with my hands?
I tie my tied shoelaces,
button my buttoned coat.

The new cemetery is spacious,
entirely future. Far, near, incessantly,
the cantors are singing.

You are quiet, a little embarrassed:
perhaps the separation will be long.
The nails are growing, slowly, sketching a truce.
The mouth cavity is at peace with its maker.

But now the earth-fists
are knocking on the boards of the trap:
let us in,
let us in.

Twenty Years in the Valley

And afterward? I don't know.
Each of us fell
into his own oblivion.

The road got wider and wider. My truck stayed
on the edge, upside-down.
At noon I sometimes look through
its burnt eyes: I don't remember
these cypress trees.
New travelers pass before us, to forget
a different war,
different dead,
faster than us.

But sometimes a wind descends to us,
rustles the wreath
that happened to roll down into the valley,
plucks one petal, then another,
tries to guess:
They love. They love not.
They love
a little. No.
A lot.
No.
Too much.

(1968)

Jason's Grave in Jerusalem

Jason, that cunning old sailor,
one of King Yannai's inner circle,
pretends that he was buried
far from the sea,
in an attractive grave in a holy city.
"Room within room he is hidden, adorned by pillars and arches;
peace and perpetual glory were carved for him in this limestone."

The grave is empty.
Only a drawing of a ship
is scratched on the wall.

Overhead, kingdoms have fallen,
new men have descended into Hades.

Not Jason. He slips away
again and again,
out of the blank wall,
in a fast ship
(cuts through the sea of air, maintaining
absolute radio-silence)
and with great profit, as always, smuggles
very expensive merchandise:
sunlight of water,
velvet of sea breeze,
marble of foam.

An Ancient Complaint

A different Holofernes says: Judith,
who put you in charge of my blood, that you presume
to belittle it? You condemn me to being forgiven
against the law.

Of all the devices of heroism, you choose
only peace. The honest handshake—
terrible is this honesty,
sharper than the sword.

So you haven't beheaded.
You abandoned the head on the neck:
a flesh statue smiling, embarrassed, upright,
a memorial to nothing.

MEMORIAL EVENING

On the evening in memory of Whatsisname, the veteran poet, I sit in the audience in the cultural center. The committee members are already seated on the podium in front of me. A long narrow table cuts them in the middle, six embarrassed faces above, twelve embarrassed shoes beneath. The opening speaker opens, says: "Honored guests, goodbye, thank you for coming. Please!" Six porters walk up onto the stage, turn the table upside down, and carefully pack the committee members inside it, each on his chair: a mass coffin. The audience has already jumped onto its feet, pushing to the exit, to the coffins that await them outside. I too shove my way through with elbows, with fists, so that I won't be late for my coffin.

CENTRAL PARK, TWILIGHT

I recognize it, but where from, this park: sugar and ice
and also a little soot in the purity. The tall buildings
rise, aloof and generous, translucent in winter calm.

Here and there, the windows—as if by chance,
yet with the distant glitter of freedom—
still reflect the receding December sun,

and already shine from inside, prepared
for the future that will spend the night here.
An old American dream of mine. And meanwhile

an old man, tall, mustached, is observing
the skaters in the rink. Grandfather?
He was never here. And I've never been.

Now on the mirror of ice, in one daring loop,
the boy glides toward me.
That cap of mine. The woolen scarf with the stripes.

Face to face, glowing with embarrassment
and already turning away, I or I
say very quickly: please don't wake up.

THE GRAND DUKE OF NEW YORK

Gabriel Preil, the Grand Duke of New York,
goes downtown incognito every day.
Disguised in a felt hat with a tiny feather,
he walks among the crowds of his subjects, listening.
The deception always succeeds: it's been fifty years
and they still haven't recognized him.
Skyscrapers built in his honor on the edges of Central Park and to
    the south
keep constant watch: where will he arrive from?
Police horses turn in every direction,
the squirrels lift up their tails: hasn't he come *yet*? And all the
    while
he's been strolling down Fifth Avenue, counting the precious
    minutes
on the gold-and-quartz watches, granting his pardon
to a couple of muggers who attacked him by mistake in some
    side street
and finally arrives
at his destination, the corner coffee shop. There he rests from his
    labors.
The waitress is suddenly radiant, she rushes up to
this loyal customer, who jokes with her sometimes
with velvet softness. But weak in faith, overworked,
she turns to ordinary people, not realizing
that out of his cup he is telling a very sweet future for her.
At twilight the Duke vanishes
down an infernal subway, crosses the river between

drawn knives, is swallowed up in a nameless apartment house,
    locks his palace,
sits down in appropriate splendor. An amber light glows for him
in a glass of Russian tea. And to make sure that the great city goes
    on living tomorrow,
he composes a special Night Proclamation which reads:

> *Beyond the shores all crime is slowly fading,*
> *And Time invites you for a friendly chat.*

EARLY WINTER, LONG ISLAND

Like the embarrassed bull that woke up in a china shop,
I stand still in this sparkling forest,
trying not to step too hard
on the thin ice that formed during the night.

But this morning there are still more surprises:
I, a stranger, feel as if I've come home,
and that wise rabbit I forgot in distant forests
is here, in a white thicket, and beckons to me, "Come on,

don't worry, it's a hard winter,
you can walk through the forest happily, calmly,
you won't disturb anything,
you won't leave even a trace."

THE DECEASED WRITER:
PHOTOGRAPH IN THE RAIN

And so, Ernie, your laughing head floats along
among black arches, in the cathedral
of an open umbrella.
I read in your wrinkles and am scared:
Storyteller, how did you guess me
before I was.

Your mustache snickers. It reconciled extremes.
You're a monk who has run away in a shabby coat
from the common sense—straight, square—of Manhattan.
You're a heretic, Ernie.
The rain is praying for your nine lives.

This finger of yours, the only thing you never doubted:
it grew up with you, typed your books.
At the end it pulled the trigger
and beckoned to you: come. Everything as foreseen.

Moments of Old Age

I

Someone asks him what day it is. What day?
He doesn't know. He's sorry; can't tell why.
The years, the people. Perhaps a different name.
He'll try to think of it, perhaps, in time.
Sometimes he finds himself outside, a stranger,
His fingers tightening around the evening paper.
Or suddenly at the market, lost in the crush
Of bodies, blue-lipped, gaping like a fish.
In the end, he'll be acquitted and go free—
An old fool who was always asking Why.

2

Stay at home: the future will not move.
A teapot waits and whistles on the stove.
The armchairs have grown thin; the faded rug
Can't understand; a stool like a dog
Lies by your slippered feet. At times a fly
From the world behind your windowpane drops by,
To fly around your head, to try the cake
You courteously offer it, to talk
About its troubles. You listen to it buzz.
No no, you don't complain that there's no peace.

The Portrait

The little boy
keeps fidgeting,
it's hard for me to catch the line
of his profile.
I draw one line
and his wrinkles multiply,
dip my brush
and his lips curl, his hair whitens,
his skin, turned blue, peels from his bones. He's gone.
The old man is gone. And I,
whither shall I go?

THE ART OF
CONTRACTION

A Small Poetics

You're allowed to write everything,
for example, *and* and *and*.
You're allowed with all the words you find,
all the meanings you plant among them.

It's a good idea, of course, to check
if the voice is your voice
and the hands are your hands.

If so, lock up your voice,
gather your hands, and obey
the voice of
the empty page.

SUGARDUKE

Grandpa masquerades as an ordinary sugar merchant. Actually he is an emperor hidden from the eyes of men, tolerant and enlightened. In his palace, camouflaged as a store, his entourage crowds around him: sacks of crystal sugar and sacks of snow sugar, boxes of cube sugar and at least ten white cones, sharp-edged, which are called sugar hats. These are the court jesters.

The years go by, and because Grandpa is tired, he puts his hand on my shoulder, appoints me his second-in-command, and bestows upon me a special title: Sugarduke. In the corner, a full sack of sugar crouches, deeply and deliciously napping, and doesn't even know what power is concealed inside it (one horsepower, but strong). I climb up onto its back, dig my heels into its ribs, and gallop forth.

After I conquer the world and liberate it, I return and announce to everyone: dear sugars, you are free from me too. I abdicate the throne of the duchy for ever and ever and anyway until evening, for we still have a mighty mission before us. The moment I finish my homework I will walk out with you, as an equal among equals, to stop the invasion of the swift and bitter tomorrow.

WALL CALENDAR

December. A polar wind, sharp-edged, new.
Angels and white bears fall into a winter sleep.
That very moment,
overhead, secretly in the soft snow
the spring traps are being set.

June. In a military ritual full of sunshine
the man is being buried at noon.
That very moment
it is midnight in the woman's belly.
The fetus is called up
and must report for active duty.

December. Suddenly the boat capsizes.
I drown in the filthy sea and, predictably,
that very moment
before my eyes all my stolen years stream past
like a sweet river.

FINAL REPORT

The findings testify to a complete disregard.
Behind the forehead
lie vast distances of blue.
The cause has not yet been determined.
Now, contrary to expectation, a suspicious
chirping begins,
and in the cage, among thin ribs,
someone wakes up: sings.

For a Literary Survey

You ask me how I write. I'll tell you, but let this be confidential. I take a ripe onion, squeeze it, dip the pen into the juice, and write. It makes excellent invisible ink: the onion juice is colorless (like the tears the onion causes), and after it dries it doesn't leave any mark. The page again appears as pure as it was. Only if it's brought close to the fire will the writing be revealed, at first hesitantly, a letter here, a letter there, and finally, as it should be, each and every sentence. There's just one problem. No one knows the secret power of the fire, and who would suspect that the pure page has anything written on it?

SILENT MOVIE

Tonight as he is lying on his back
the blank ceiling turns into a movie screen
through the shutters oblique light shines
destinies, black and white

The mother kisses the child and is gone
the child runs after her climbs the wall
encounters a cake comes out with a whipped-cream face
the father affable and elegant across the ocean

The film stops for a moment years pass
soon for them all a happy ending
he feels close to them since they're total strangers
he himself stays on in the dark

Meanwhile dawn rises the ceiling is empty
now he will shut his eyes and watch
the repeat performance
projected on the inside of his eyelids

THE ART OF CONTRACTION

At first he thinks the entire meadow in its abundance belongs to him, with all its thousands of green surprises. Then he realizes that he can't bear such chaos. True, the grass blades aren't very high, they reach no farther than his knees, maybe just his ankles, and yet they are a labyrinth, twisted, deceptive. There is not a single path, and thus an infinity of paths: free to choose any direction he wishes, he is irretrievably lost.

Well then, he chooses contraction. Not a meadow, but a patch of lawn. Not even that, but three blades of grass. Not three, not even one (and this, he feels, is the crux of the matter), not even a single blade of grass, but the picture of one. This is the essence.

Finally, after he hangs it on the wall, he understands: this painted blade of grass, which implies the entire meadow, also denies the entire meadow.

SOMINEX

The old radio, its dial showing all the names of the cities, glows again in the dark. I didn't know it was still alive. Well then, I'm still young. The cities, enchanted and distant again, sing for me, give me the news of the years.

The door opens. Who is coming to see me, I'm coming to see me, to take me away. Look, it's hard to talk in one person, let's go back to you-and-me, the way we used to, all right? We'll have to leave in a moment, but there's nothing to be scared of, really there isn't. Before we finish, here is the weather report: it will be cold tomorrow. You're taking a scarf? Take it, take it, if it makes you feel any better.

The body you leave: they'll freeze it for a day or two, then (for an exorbitant fee) they'll wash it, diaper it, make a large baby. Then they'll call your son to identify Daddy among those other babies waiting to go back into Mommy's belly. You're laughing. But it's from the Bible, that amazing verse in the Book of Job: "Naked I came from my mother's womb, and naked I shall return thither." What does it mean, "return thither"? Have you ever thought about that?

And here's an urgent report that we've just received at the news desk: we are now closing down for the night. Just one more minute before we leave. Look, this calm head, these relaxed, open hands—I never imagined that this moment could be so kind.

CONVERSATION

Four talked about the pine tree. One defined it by genus, species, and variety. One assessed its disadvantages for the lumber industry. One quoted poems about pine trees in many languages. One took root, stretched out branches, and rustled.

April

A nameless lavender, a lavender of April.
To drift unheard in the good mist,
to return by a thread
into the heart of the lavender moss from which I came
with what name, with what breath.

The End of Winter

Gentle snowman,
with your coal eyes you foresaw black events,
a black future. What courage was reflected from your eyes:
not even one blink! And in the middle
the nose is still there, sticking out: the pessimistic carrot.
Rejoice, young man, in your senility.
True, you and I at the end of winter
are a bit smaller, frailer,
but you know as well as I do:
beautiful were the days of my winter, of your winter,
and our summer will be beautiful too.
Why should we wait for it in a back yard?
Let's sneak away from here, now,
before the mud of spring,
let's cheerfully and nimbly flow down the street and onward
to the wide sea, if it exists.
Tomorrow the radio will announce
that not a trace of us has been found, forever.

TOWARD HOME

ACROBATICS

A first drumroll—and he is a coil of air, his limbs four rubber snakes, he whirls, descends in a wide arc, lands on one fingertip. Very nice, but nothing new.

A second drumroll—and he is a ball among seven balls, kicking, being kicked, descends in a wide arc, catches them all on his nose. Very nice, but nothing new.

Suddenly, quite unforeseen, his feet are standing on the stage, above them his hips, his belly, chest, shoulders, neck, and at the top: his face, turned serenely toward the darkness. There is no greater art.

BRIDGEHEAD PHOTOGRAPH

In sun and snow, peacefully, it slumbers,
this Brooklyn from another world,
between huge soft eiderdown quilts
of Sabbath.

In front of me the bridge, high up
on thin translucent ice-threads, is suspended
in doubt. From here to the skyline
nothing is moving but my breath.

No hurry. On the wharf opposite:
a sign, Dead End.
It has several meanings,
all simple.

For seventy years now I've stood at this bridgehead
with the heavy box camera on its tripod.
My hands underneath the black cloth are still waiting
for the perfect light.

As if there were still
that Jewish snow. The glare
dazzles me, the exposure
is too wide. Nothing will appear on the photo

but a white rectangle.
And this is no metaphor, truly, this is
the matter itself,
just as I

finally break away, heading home. Following me,
gray and white and cheerful, a row of seagulls
waddle along: Lubavitcher hasidim. They wave good-bye and
        vanish,
like me, in the snow.

DEVOTION

Rubber gloves, for the kitchen—brutish, efficient; for the surgeon's table—oily, gossiping, searching into the most intimate details, and finally, disinfected.

Of all rubber gloves there is only one that is noble: the eternal one that does not exist, the glove in De Chirico's painting *Song of Love*. It is pinned to a bare, whitewashed wall; beneath it an unfathomable ball is dreaming; and beside it, on the wall, a plaster head of a man, perhaps of Apollo, blindly stares into space. The head does not know that far behind, in antispace, a black locomotive is puffing away, sprouting a cloud, and it is evening already. But the glove hangs here, in front of us, with utter devotion, and with all its limp fingers it points downward and shows us, shows us the way.

FOR HOW LONG

Snow, you are disregarding me,
gradually being forgotten,
where shall I leave you
my breath, my feet?
A great tranquillity used to welcome us.
Have you forgotten? You who erase footprints,
now that I have grown old like you, do not forsake me.

Out of Line

Lines in a poem, long ones, short ones: each bound to its allotted end.
But we, out of line, fly about in space, return, ignite at the air's edge,
burn out, spread darkness all around us.

HE'LL COME OUT FOR SURE

"Out, out,
   push some more, lady,
   he can't help it, he'll come out for sure."

The sharp air bursts into him,
   again bursts out of his mouth:
   "Mommy Mommy Ah me Mommy."

He sums up this whole long complaint
   in one sound:
   "Eeeeeee . . ."

In the huge nauseating space where he's floating,
   he finds a first grip on things,
   finger-handcuffs around his ankles:

the midwife lifts him, head downward,
   his tiny arms hanging to the side,
   a reverse crucifixion.

Only after a moment of eternity
   arrives the angel, that veteran clerk,
   checking the ID number

and with great mercy, according to standard procedure,
   slaps him on the mouth
   and helps him forget.

Now everything is again soft and warm, again womb,
and from a great distance he hears
a first, kindhearted, jovial sentence:

"A healthy boy, lady, and strong too,
bellowing like an ox,
mazal tov."

THE RUNNER ARTIST

The loneliness
of the short-distance runner.

His breath holds out only
till the halfway mark.

Only his footprints
follow him devotedly.

Go! Only two contestants:
right leg and left leg.

So there's no winner, no loser.
He's allowed to sit down and rest,

to go home, or, if he wants to, he's even
allowed to run.

Picture Postcard
from Our Youth

On your piano a plaster Beethoven stands
and thinks: Thank goodness I've gone deaf.
Even the neighborhood sparrows are singing out of tune this
    morning.

Only the Kurdish peddler is being true to himself
as he limps along the street shouting *Old clothes!*
in his bargain-basement Hebrew.

It doesn't matter. From the tangle of voices, the one voice ascends.
A blue bell of air
arches above us.

TOWARD HOME

Night, and my wristwatch is slow. It's the wrist's fault. I sit at the edge of the roof and ask (whom?) how I can reach. It depends, crawling or jumping? Once there were steps here, close to the wall, which climbed from the yard to the roof. There is still a remnant of them, a zigzag of plaster, just a remnant. Well, there's no choice: I have to jump. I crouch down close to the wall, try to rub my shoulders against the plaster so I won't fall, and fall.

In the corner of the yard the well is still waiting for me, square, heavy with an iron lid. Up above, on the tower of the Lutheran church, a lunar clock hovers: it has despaired of me and given up on both its hands. I didn't realize I was that late.

Now that everything is lost, a great calm descends upon me. The well is dozing, the iron lid echoes with the huge silence. I lift it carefully: in the circle of water, close to me, a lunar face is floating. I recognize it from somewhere. If I go into it deeply enough, surely I will remember from where.

Outside an Air Base,
California

On the bottom of this ocean of air which aeons ago
invaded and drove away the ocean,
I stand,
an in-between creature among the developing species.

The last train, a haggard iron monster, still
crawls among small rocks toward its end,
and on the waves of cloud above me the Zeppelin, that primeval
    whale,
still floats serenely. Gleams and vanishes.

I'm late. New species evolve continually.
The predatory plane in the sky. It has run out of time.
An instant shadow, unidentified, snatches from it
a wasted microsecond.

My body, exposed to radar, is surrounded by data.
THIS AREA IS OUT OF BOUNDS, the sign admonishes me,
KEEP OUT.
YOU HAVE BEEN WARNED.

I retrace my steps,
which meanwhile have turned to stone.
And for secret reasons that I can't analyze here,
I'm happy I have existed.

A New Lover

You pick me up, a coin someone has lost,
and rub me between thumb and forefinger.
I try to be new, even to shine a little.

You look for my denomination,
examine the face stamped on me.
I make myself rare, almost a real king.

Still not enough. You incline a doubtful ear,
strike me, and listen. I ring for you
with my purest sound, almost flawless.

And last, as an experienced money changer,
you bite me: perhaps it will bend,
this phony gold piece.

But I am hard, I stand the test; not gold, but still
a decent alloy. Reassured,
now you can spend me, at your will.

SUDDEN HEART

Sudden heart, tightrope walker with no rope
and no rest, how long will it be?
Down in the lighted arena the horses shake their heads
over you, their bright plumes waving good-bye.
And already the mournful tuba
and that sentimental codger, the double bass,
lament you in a syncopated rhythm.
Far down below,
to meet your fall, stretches
the drum.

But this blue void,
this free fall,
this piercing joy

THE FREEDOM
MACHINE

Exposure

The skin mask,
underneath it
the flesh mask,
underneath *it* the
skull-bones, and
the black spaces
between galaxies.

POINT OF DEPARTURE

Hidden in the study at dusk,
I wait, not yet lonely.
A heavy walnut bureau opens up the night.
The clock is a tired sentry,
its steps growing faint.

From where? In Grandfather's typewriter,
an Underwood from ancient times,
thousands of alphabets are ready.
What tidings?

I think that not everything is in doubt.
I follow the moment, not to let it slip away.
My arms are rather thin.
I am nine years old.

Beyond the door begins
the interstellar space which I'm ready for.
Gravity drains from me like colors at dusk.
I fly so fast that I'm motionless
and leave behind me
the transparent wake of the past.

The Limits of Physics

In the deep armchair, the boy sits motionless.
The universe obeys laws.
November, powdered graphite, passes
yellowing in the cloud, glimmering
in the challenge of sulfur.

In the armchair, the boy sits.
The lightning rod waits on his head, motionless.
The brass glitters.
The iron filings swirl in the magnetic field
and rise, somewhat obliquely, to their fate.
The boy, motionless, sits in the magnetic field.

Now the cloud whitens. The brass telescope
(it's also called a spyglass)
catches it easily.
The universe obeys laws in a dry rustle
like falling leaves (but more silent).
Thus cold electricity sparkles
when you rub amber with silk.

In all this there is a great consolation, but
suddenly in a gap of the cloud
a wheel of swallows
bursts
from a wheel of swallows.

The boy is alive,
alive, bursting,
waving himself out of himself.
All laws obey him at once:
his fall
is free.

THE STORY

Once I read a story
about a grasshopper one day old,
a green adventurer who at dusk
was swallowed up by a bat.

Right after this the wise old owl
gave a short consolation speech:
Bats also have the right to make a living,
and there are many grasshoppers still left.

Right after this came
the end: an empty page.

Forty years now have gone by.
Still leaning above that empty page,
I do not have the strength
to close the book.

THE FREEDOM MACHINE

In the cage of the Siberian snow fox,
a distinguished prisoner,
they have installed the freedom machine.

It is a drum-shaped iron wheel 30 inches across,
with a rim 12 inches wide;
on the rim there are pegs for the feet,
and the wheel's axle is fastened to the wall.

Whenever the Siberian fox gets tired
he jumps in
and starts running.
The freedom machine rolls out
a dizzying path
for his four hundred legs
which move like the wind
under his yearning body
back
to the farthest North.

They oil the wheel once a week.

How To

The death mask is prepared
from the negative of the face.
After the soul has left, cover
the face with soft clay,
then peel it off, slowly.
In it, you get a large mold:
instead of the nose a hole,
instead of the eyesockets two blobs.
Now pour the plaster, premixed,
into the mold, wait
till it hardens,
then separate the parts:
in the positive, the nose juts out again,
the eyesockets collapse. Now
take the plaster face
and cover your face of flesh with it
and live.

RECOGNITION

In the last room in our house,
at the edge of a wondrously curled cloud,
a Chinese rider raced by on his horse,
out of breath, embroidered in silk.

He raced and he raced from China, trying to arrive.
As the years passed, he slanted toward me
reproachful glances. I would have gone to meet him,
but the distance was very great.

And now, when I no longer know whether
he dissolved in the cloud or burned down with the house,
I realize that we were both wrong and that
we were one, embroidered in each other.

Visit to a Physicist

On the blackboard in his study, time
is calculated, in a long formula
that tends toward zero.

He's restless. While he offers me coffee
and small talk, he keeps glancing stealthily
at the formula's end,

gets up, grabs a sponge, erases, leaves
the correct conclusion:
an empty blackboard.

He smiles apologetically as he walks back
to the table. But we both know what happened:
time has been proved a fallacy: nothing more.

Now we sit face to face.
He reads in my eyes
the history of stars long dead,

and in his translucent skull, as in a crystal
ball, I foresee
this moment.

Failure

And one
who a hundred years ago
failed the math test
and is afraid to go home.

Chalk face, eyes of ink.
Locked behind the bars
of the notebook pages
and dripping with red mistakes.

As punishment, he's copied the right answer
a hundred times on the blackboard.
He already knows that one divided by zero
tends to infinity.

Still: he gets an F.

Among the empty wooden benches
opposite the stained map of the world
he's hiding from the janitor, who might come
and bring him to life.

But even if he returned to the world of lies,
he'll never forget the answer
just as he remembered it all the years of his death
until now.

Sport

I never learned to swim. In shallow waters
among seaweed, I somehow manage to
float. Even large waves curl
into life belts for me. But why?

Actually, I don't need water to swim in. Only at home
can I reveal what a great champion I am.
Crawl or breaststroke or butterfly—any style:
eel-like I go slithering from kitchen to bathtub

and break all the records of myself,
win the cup and slowly savor the champagne.
But what's this, my good angel is stirring,
he lectures and finally shouts:

"What chutzpah it is to swim among the drowned,
and you make this into a sport? For shame!"
He's right: there is a time to return. I flick on the news,
dive into the radio waves, and drown.

BISECTION

Asymmetrical face. Half of it
drawn in the cave at Altamira
before the buffalo hunt. Half
designed by computer.
One sharp vertical crease
bisecting the forehead
keeps them apart.

Wind from Variable Directions

1

I am as yet
a storm of zero force.
Almost a breath.

2

Around and around
whirling in my cycles,
perhaps in vain.

3

The window is open
onto the vast inner distances
between cupboard and table.
I steal in, breathe,
fill the curtain like a sail,
travel inward, arrive
with great
love.

4

Sometimes, now for example,
I am a light breeze from the south
or near-south. Before dawn
I drift through the pine needles,
make off through the woods,
swerve, suddenly.

No one relies on me, I know.
A tense army of quicksilver sentries,
of pressure-pointers,
spies on me, interprets me, guesses
what I will turn into next
and with what fierceness.

But why?
All my directions are obvious:
driven by horror of the void
I pounce
on the void.

5
South. Sand pyramids shift in search of the grave.
Suddenly, erect, the jasmine hand, shining.

West. Ocean, iodine and pale green gall.
Suddenly, tidings of sulfur betraying the horizon.

North. Shuttered sky. A town of onion and a town of soot.
Suddenly, a star, divine, sharp-eyed, of snow.

East.

6
Old maps used to draw me
as a baby-faced cherub. I am all contraries:
four or eight baby faces
with puffed-out cheeks, blowing against each other
from the world's corners to its core.

But at this moment, before summer,
I spin all the points of the compass
like a toy weathervane.

7

Second childhood, or third,
from south-southeast:
I turn the street upside down
(the man, scared: where is my hat?
the hat, scared: where is my head?)

And here, still,
the house, grown so old.
I knock on the empty window and wait
impatiently:
who?

Then, the park, the pond.
I blow carefully
on the paper boats.
New children run after me. How easy
to catch me with empty hands.

8

Every country gives me a name of its own:
Sirocco, Hamsin, Boreas.
My name disappears in my names.

I don't care, really I don't.
My place is whither,
my return is when.

9

A day solid as glass:
glass sea, glass sky,
and the seagull crucified in the middle.
And the sailboat stopped
at the bottleneck.

This too is just an illusion,
a deceptive calm:
the snake of air
coiled round and round
lies in wait for
its own tail.

10

Driven by horror of the void, I
whistle in the forest, breathe through the cracks of the wall,
whisper in paper.
In the abundance of hair I am even allowed to be silent.
It is only repose that I'm not allowed,
and I resign myself.
Well then, dear friends, I have passed. Am no more.
Good-bye to you all,
the far and the even farther.

11

Now that winter erupts,
just before I split into storms,
I steal a moment
and dream, quickly,

of the eternal calm of
the air bubble
trapped in glass.

12

North and northwest are harsh masters.
I have been recalled,
legions upon legions of air.
I gather my forces on the slope
(grass runs over grass)
I rise
(the abandoned newspaper
flaps, heralds my coming)
I arrive
in the darkness of noon.
A sharp ray cuts
a hole in the cloud,
points out the targets:
a pale wall,
a city of paper.
But in the eye of the hurricane,
silence.
The lit candle, the calm golden flame.

A storm of zero force.
Almost a breath.

a pale wall,
a city of paper.
But in the eye of the hurricane,
silence.
The lit candle, the calm golden flame.

A storm of zero force.
Almost a breath.

PREVIOUS LIVES

Epilogue to Robinson Crusoe

From a parrot-heavy and speech-forsaken island
he returned, as if yesterday he were waiting
till a good wind came. He returned and here he is.
But at the door all the years suddenly
turned on their hinge.
                              And then,
between hollow armchairs he knew
what had come to pass in the meantime, and grew wise
like somebody who has no return before him.
Too wise to live, dried out and gray he remained
with the pipe of his stories, and talked—
so as to silence the ticking of his dead
and their alarms—he talked and talked
about an island that would never enter history.

THE TOWER

I did not want to grow, but quick-fingered memories
put layer upon layer, each one alone,
and were mixed in the tumult of strange tongues
and left in me unguarded entrances,
stairs that led nowhere,
perspectives that were broken.
Finally, I was abandoned.
Only sometimes in the twisted corridor
a small speechless whisper
still rises in me and runs
like a draft and it seems to me
that I am a whirlwind
whose head is for a moment in the sky
and before I wake up
the mass of my burnt bricks crumbles
and turns back
to clay.

PAGES IN AN ALBUM

Destined to great things, he lies on his belly and confidently
sucks. The expanses of the floor await him:
everything is a target; he can't miss. And already
he's grown up, standing on his feet and forgetting
what he will never learn.
For a moment he enters a class picture and smiles
on the top row, next to the teacher. Meanwhile
with a woman or two, on the beach, footprints
vanishing in the sand. At this time he is already resting,
adult and slightly yellowing, in a serious pose,
hand upon forehead, twilight. Even before he has found a solution,
he goes on cautiously in the dim corridor, like a thief,
and at the end finds
himself, waiting for himself in the mirror:
the too bright light
of a flashbulb catches
his image
and burns out
the glass lenses of his eyes.

SEASHELL

Coiled into myself, I was not a seashell for your voice.
I will remain on the unsteady sand.
If a passerby happened to pick me up,
to try me as an ear, to listen in me for good news
of the sea—I didn't say a word.
With murmuring, with delusive silence,
I gave him back the wide-awake beat
of his blood. As if I had sung: as if he had heard.
Emptier than ever, imprisoned in my convolutions,
how will I live by the commands that you didn't give me,
and on what shore, to what rest's end?
I remain on the shifting sand.
I have no escape from your silence.

COME

Come out of your astrology, the order
of constellations imprisoned in wheels
which shone, but not for you.
The sign of Libra is balanced.
You are tired. Your gaze ascending
to distances which you do not find
returns empty into your eyes.
Come: and be gathered into the midst of the darkness
between the stars, and revolve,
extinguished, inside the wheel of your blood.

THE SHOT

Upside-down, he still
waits, and in his ears there is still
just the beginning of a sound,
like the one syllable
of death, an echo
rebounding inside his skull.
A dry drizzle escapes
from the sandbags. A wind
waves the hair and surrenders.
But still he can command
his body's troops, he gives the signal
and the revolution of his eyeballs turns
inward, now he can see:
well then,
a time to keep silence.
He will marshal himself again,
hide in the grass,
lie in ambush
for the things to come.
But his refugee blood
which wandered about in his veins
cannot be imprisoned,
leaves too soon
and cries out from the ground,
the ground which did not open its mouth
and did not want to be his.

The Beginning

In the ice-filled chaos before the end of creation,
distant fleets of steel are waiting.
Boundaries are secretly marked.
High above the smoke and the odor of fat and skins hovers
a yellow magnetic stain;
oblique rays at the pole, alert, quick-eyed,
search for the signal. The code is cracked.
Now that all is prepared for darkness,
a wind, with savage fur, from the horizon, blows
in the hollow bones of mountains,
and at the zero hour
the Great Bear, blazing, strides forth
in heat. The heavens stand now,
and the earth, and all their hosts.
A time of war.

The Cycle

Go to the ant, you sluggard, and go
in the black column between mountain-high furrows
in the way of all your kind
and store the harvest of one grain. Thus
to dust you will return in a crumbling season,
to the deep cells of larvae,
to the blind milk-white mass
wriggling with desire
to swarm, to run
in the black column between mountain-high furrows
and in an autumn wind
to store the harvest of one grain which will come
and the straw that is your body.
Consider your ways.

Harvests

The prudent field mouse
hoards and hoards for the time of battle and siege.
His home is furnished with cunning
passageways; his granary is full.
Above him,
as always, the fire revels in the wheat
and in the heart of the sun, waiting for him—
sharp-eyed, punctual—the hawk.

Ready for Parting

Ready for parting, as if my back were turned,
I see my dead come toward me, transparent and breathing.
I do not consent:
one walk around the square, one rain,
and I am another, with imperfect rims, like clouds.
Gray in the passing town, passing and glad,
among transitory streetlamps,
wearing my strangeness like a coat, I am free to stand
with the people who stand at the opening of a moment
in a chance doorway, anonymous as raindrops
and, being strangers, near and flowing one into another.

Ready for parting, waiting awhile
for the signs of my life which appear in the chipped plaster
and look out from the grimy windowpane. A surprise of roses.
Bursting out and already future, twisted into its veins—
a blossoming to every wind. Perhaps
not in my own time into myself and from myself and onward
from gate within gate I will go out into the jungle of rain,
free to pass on like one who has tried his strength
I will go out
from the space in between as if from the walls of denial.

Scarabs

At noon you go back to the dust
of cities plowed and harvested and uncover potsherds
from the sockets of their eyes. Now, in what century,
according to what broken calendar, passes before you
the rider who crumbled in the wind,
and returns to the harvest of arrows and swords, like you.
Astonished in the wind of ashes,
he bends the empty bow of his eyebrows, searches
for treasures of gold and straw.

All is left undecided. And begins forever
in the dust where—black, speechless—
scarabs,
with all their feet,
knead bricks for the walls and storehouses
of treasure cities,
and the blood splashes in the clay.

ALREADY

Already I was before I am
forced in a surprised night wind to return
exhausted in dry grass and obeying
the command of a nagging voice.
On the main road bright candles for the dead
told me to come:
the house, the strange name lying in wait for me
in these veins of darkness. Closed
between my blood and my blood, in the blind warmth
folded inside me, kicking from within me to leave
the sweet hollow and suddenly cry out
in the air running through the lungs.
Already I am not
(I was a distant summer) and at this moment,
when I must see the other light, I am
that I am. Already
I do not remember.

BRAIN

Brain

1

In the dark night of the skull
he suddenly discovers
he's born.

A difficult moment.

Since then he's been very busy.
He thinks
that he thinks that
and he goes around and around:
where's the way out?

If, in some world, there were things,
he of course would love them very much,
he would give names to them all.
For instance: Brain.
That's me. Brain. I'm it.

Ever since his exile, he reasons:
there must have been a place to rest.

2

How will he move the darkness?

Brain hovers upon the face of the deep.
But now two deep wounds burst
in the bones of the forehead. Eyes.

The eyes betray to him
the world: here, spread out before him,
a world, complete, solid:
look, Brain is hovering
just five feet six inches above the floor!
Now that the truth is out
he is overwhelmed by vertigo:
five feet six!
Alone upon the face of the deep.

3
He has a suspicion
that in the whole universe of the skull
there is no other brain but him.

Then, a new suspicion:
that myriads of brains are imprisoned in him,
packed together,
splitting off from him, betraying him from within,
surrounding him.

And he doesn't know which evil
is the lesser.

4
True, he's not handsome, but
he's interesting-looking:
grayish white convolutions,
a bit oily, sliding back and forth.
Silver curls inside the skull?

Oh no, Brain resembles
nothing else in the world,
except perhaps
the small intestine.

5

This is a mountain.
This is a woman.
But immediately Brain deciphers:
Not a mountain. An upside-down valley.
Not a woman. A body putting up a front.
Only the cave fever
gripping the blood
is still the same desire.

6

Brain makes a friend, a shut-in like himself.
They both have radio sets
and in their spare time
they broadcast to each other from the attic.
Brain asks, for example:
Have you got syllogisms? Alarm centers?
Six hundred million memory cells?
And how do you feel inside your cranium, Brain?

Sometimes he jokes around:
Have you heard any good ones lately?
Have you seen any good ones, Brain,
have you smelled any, tasted any?
(And all along he knows his sixth sense

is the most sensational of the five.)
But his friend is upset:
You're getting on my nerves, Brain.

After a while he becomes really intimate with him
and broadcasts some strictly personal problems:
Tell me, do you know how to forget?

7
One of his fears: that he still has hieroglyphs
carved inside him.
He is the twisted brain
of Pharaoh on his deathbed.
Pharaoh is not yet ready.
Before they mummify him
they pierce both his nostrils
and suck out
the cold contents of his skull.

8
Midway into my death, in bitter grief
About my life's midway, being still ensnared
In a bush of veins, dark, with no relief,

In a bush of veins, still waiting for the word,
There suddenly burst out, before I knew,
This blood of mine, my servant and my lord—

Why did I speak. Whom did I speak to. No,
It wasn't this I wanted to announce.
Hello? Who's there, who's listening? Hello?

9

The internal veins of the head extend to the brain's anterior base;
from these radiate the veins of the proencephalon, the mesenceph-
alon, and the metencephalon. The brain shell, although it is very thin
(very), contains the great majority of the neurons in the nervous sys-
tem (in man, approximately 10 billion). The brain is the organ of
time. A dog from which the cerebrum has been removed is still able
to live for a time, but only in the present. All the doggish past van-
ishes instantly, and the doggish future already does not exist.
Brain yawns: he is embarrassed by so much praise.
Those marvelous symbols! Who invented them?
Brain. And the paper? Brain.
And me?
But Brain has learned to evade
such attacks.
He gives a sign: Let there be darkness!
And at once
the fingers shut the encyclopedia.

10

He would like to be faithful
only to himself,
to be pure and void,
void of memory like a mirror.

11

He is a moon whose *two* sides
are forever dark.

[149

12

Brain counts
seconds on his journey from one star to the next.
Years on his journey from one grain of sand to the next.
Aeons on his longest journey: to Brain.

13

A time of peace. He pampers himself a bit
by thinking
that far away, somewhere in outer space,
in some unguessed-at nebula,
between the stars that melt to milky haze,
some Purpose is waiting for him—still obscure,
but his, entirely his. Tomorrow, or
the day after tomorrow (who can tell?),
he may strip off his somber prison clothes,
and in a nutshell
blithely he'll take off, and fly, and land:
the sovereign of worlds without end.

14

Brain gropes around: he is surrounded.
No refuge in the skull.
Inside the maze twists
the maze.

Brain is now enormous: a gray cloud,
a very heavy cloud. In the throat of this cloud
sticks
a jagged lightning bolt.

Wait a second: Brain hears himself
ticking off the seconds.
A time bomb?
He wasn't ready for that.
He was off his guard.

But Brain shakes himself free
and declares: I'm just a dream.

15

Brain receives signals
through immense distances.
From space, from a depth dark-years away,
a living code reaches him,
another world broadcasting without cease, like himself,
without sleep, like himself,
without knowledge.

A heart?

16

Brain, pleased, surveys his centers:
a center for speech, a center for lies,
a center for memory
(seventy clocks, at least, each keeping its own time),
a special center for pain—
Who is speaking, please? Who's there?
Suddenly he hears the astounding news:
There is a hidden circle somewhere
whose center is everywhere
and whose circumference is nowhere;

a center which is so near
that he will never
be able
to see it.

17

Now he sees what is to come:
he will depart slowly, reluctantly,
and in some disorder.
First
his fear deserts him.

Then he is without the sarcasm,
the joking around,
the puns.
Then his conjectures are disconnected.
He lingers on for a while: something was here once,
very near, a nuisance. What could it have been—

Then he no longer has to remember.

Then
he is quite forgotten,

and he is light.

END OF THE QUESTIONNAIRE

Housing conditions: number of galaxy and star,
number of grave.
Are you alone or not.
What grass grows on top of you,
and from where (e.g., from your stomach, eyes, mouth, etc.).

You have the right to appeal.

In the blank space below, state
how long you have been awake and why you are surprised.

ACKNOWLEDGMENTS

Most of these translations were done in consultation with Dan Pagis.

After his death, Chana Kronfeld generously guided me through the following: "Ein Leben," "An Opening to Satan," "Tidings," "Writers," "Real-Life Story," "A Moment at the Louvre," "An Ancient Complaint," "A Small Poetics," "Sugarduke," "Final Report," "For a Literary Survey," "Conversation," "April," "The End of Winter," "For How Long," "He'll Come Out for Sure," "Picture Postcard from Our Youth," "Toward Home," and "Epilogue to Robinson Crusoe."

I am also grateful to the National Endowment for the Arts for their financial support.

ABOUT THE AUTHOR

DAN PAGIS was born in 1930 in Bukovina (formerly part of Austria, then Romania, now Russia). During the Second World War he spent three years in a Nazi concentration camp. In 1946 he went to Israel, learned Hebrew, and became a teacher in a kibbutz. He settled in Jerusalem in 1956 and obtained a doctorate from the Hebrew University, where for many years he was professor of medieval Hebrew literature. He also taught at the Jewish Theological Seminary in New York, Harvard, and the University of California at San Diego and at Berkeley. His books of poems are *The Shadow Dial* (1959), *Late Leisure* (1964), *Transformation* (1970), *Brain* (1975, 1977), *Twelve Faces* (1981), *Double Exposure* (1983), and *Last Poems* (1987). His scholarly works include *The Poetry of David Vogel* (1966; 4th ed., 1975), *The Poetry of Levi Ibn Altabban of Saragossa* (1968), *Secular Poetry and Poetic Theory—Moses Ibn Ezra and His Contemporaries* (1970), *Change and Tradition: Hebrew Poetry in Spain and Italy* (1976), and *The Riddle* (1986). Dan Pagis died on July 29, 1986.

Design by David Bullen
Typeset in Mergenthaler Granjon
by Wilsted & Taylor
Printed by Maple-Vail
on chlorine- and acid-free paper